Rare Momentum

ATHENA KILDEGAARD was born in Wyoming, grew up in Minnesota, and has lived in Sydney Australia, Chicago, Austin Texas, Oxford Mississippi, New Orleans, and Guanajuato Mexico. She now lives in Morris out west there a ways in Minnesota where she directs a non-profit cultural organization, is a roster artist with COMPASS/Writers and Artists in the Schools, and occasionally teaches at the University of Minnesota, Morris. Her poems have appeared widely in such journals as *Poetry East*, *Faultline*, *The Malahat Review*, *Puerto del Sol*, *The Seattle Review*, and elsewhere.

D1003826

ATHENA KILDEGAARD

Rare Momentum

PREFACE *by* John Calvin Rezmerski

Athena Kildegaard

Red Dragonfly Press :: 2006

Grateful acknowledgment goes to *Wind* for publishing six of these poems.

Profound thanks to my parents and John Rezmerski who opened the door.

ISBN-13: 978-1-890193-65-2
ISBN-10: 1-890193-65-8

Printed in the United States of America
by BookMobile

The cover painting is by Michael Eble
('Apprentice's Day Off,' oil on canvas)

Typeset in Figural 11.25 / 20
a digital adaptation of type designed by Oldrich Menhart

Published by Red Dragonfly Press
press-in-residence at the Anderson Center
P. O. Box 406
Red Wing, MN 55066
www.reddragonflypress.org

for Arne

Momentum

Vestige

Preface

Poems written according to the numerical scheme known as the Fibonacci sequence have been around for centuries (even way before Fibonacci). They've been a staple in some creative writing classes since sometime in the 1970s. Recently, they've become a game, a fad, a craze on the World Wide Web, prompted by Gregory K. Pincus, who nicknamed them "fibs." They seem poised to rival cinquains and haiku as anyone-can-do-it verse exercises. Anyone can do it, sort of—but just as a good haiku requires more than merely counting syllables, so does a good "fib."

Athena Kildegaard earned her poetic stripes way before the fib fad. As a consequence this collection is well described by its title, Rare Momentum. In her hands, the Fibonacci sequence is neither a formal stunt, nor stunted by formality, but is an opportunity to present vitally compressed feeling within a formal structure which is at once constrained and expansive. The seven-line structure, ending in a line of thirteen syllables, holds in check the opportunity to go on to 21, then 34, etc. However, it it is not really about numbers, but about a kind of recursiveness that numbers reveal. The poems let us begin with an act as simple as a kiss, to "enfold, unfold, a working through and against, again," eventually becoming "a prayer for immortality: blessings on your tongue." Abstract numerical structure is enlisted in the service of sense, sensuousness, and sensuality, "just the way milk loves / a saucer."

Kildegaard never surrenders to sentimentality; her poems are rooted in experience, unafraid to confront death or "The ugly dirge of / power played by big red hands." Unlike cinquains which often provide mere reports, or haiku which focus on brilliant moments of revealed feeling—or "fibs" that don't do anything more—these Fibonacci poems typically sweep us along toward the rewards of emotional complexity .

—John Calvin Rezmerski
August 2006

Momentum

Kiss
me
again
tongue and lips
like Fibonacci's
sequence, each movement a spiral,
enfold, unfold, a working through and against, again.

Ear
hear
the rare
momentum
time out of time, no
shadow only light whipping
itself into frenzies of red-tailed hawk and snow goose.

Borne
by
willow
the sparrow's
nest gathers itself
into a hand of narrow grass
cupped around what only mind weaves through its opening.

Luck

wears

a crown

of lace dew.

The spider drowns in

morning. We'll stroke where stroking's due

and hope for light, rearrange the day, we'll knock on wood.

I
eye
look now
Narcissus
tipped on water's edge
the strider has pulled our shadow
and the sun moves. You are not you nor we together.

So
dry
the day
that opens
in loneliness, hour
before the rain, minute without
tears. Sigh no more, lady. Open your gold parasol.

Sun

rise

before

dreams eclipse

desires. Or here

I am standing in the dark, pen

pulling me like a half-moon chariot through to dawn.

Earth—
I
love that
warm and soft
across the palate.
My mouth barely opens for its
escape. But what a portal when earth returns for me.

Still
life
burgeons:
cool pitcher,
figs and ripe cheese wedged
to the core, light reflected on
a spoon's belly, a pigeon flopped open like a whore.

All

I

wanted

was friction—

my body lit up

by a stranger (yes)—long after

the last tip—whose pick-up hood wasn't yet hot to touch.

All
told—
sprung glass,
hood of night,
the criminal gone—
I stood bound and spelled, unable
to guess at what world had just spilled its nerve at my feet.

One
dead
today.
One: enough.
Last night my son sang
America the Beautiful,
tried the descant, then showed me his almost perfect wings.

11/9/03

One
pulse
loosed from
the mooring
of the heart and you're
lost. Two and time stands still. Love storms
the wide horizon and reason leaves a narrow wake.

At

two

o'clock

I love you

just the way milk loves

a saucer. And ten hours later

you slip into my dreams, a lithe, hungry animal.

Be-
hold
nation
of warriors
tramping old vineyards.
Wrath dies on the vine. Come around
the goblet, pass, before we've lost the need to be held.

Geese

guide

storm clouds

over lost

top soil, eroded

banks, the last farmer's disaster,

fenceposts askew. No deluge will balance what man soiled.

Bones:

how

many

of you lie

below the surface,

undisturbed, disturbing in your

insistence that we listen to the lies of our past.

Once
born
lucky,
twice with pride.
The ugly dirge of
power played by big red hands. Who
can listen to this and not admit to fear or shame?

Ooh

la

ooh la

la la, loop

or frond, boa-long,

twist and turn, seed, pod, pollen, spore,

borne on wind this song without a verse to bear it down.

There

is

no god.

No, I say.

Only the wonder.

Why do worms rise to rain? For me
only light will do, cleansing, sourceless, won and winning.

Snow

clings

below

black branches.

Oh to be swept up!

Our skis follow where others cut

a path here straight here angled toward the frozen lake.

I
work
alone.
The silence
swarms. Do you hear? These
bees of solitude hang their nests
from my neck, aortic, adroit, goddamn them all.

One

thing

I hid

(fake gold ring)

because I wasn't

allowed a boyfriend, not friend but

boy who wrote "my true love witch is you." I hid my broom.

True

rose?

Lost now

the formal

blueprint of amour—

Mister Lincoln, Queen Bess, fame

and fidelity, no regrets rose, please, no regrets.

Sough

sough

wind, worn

hieroglyph

of time, the now and

now and now ever coming, sign

for ineradicable, for found and lost, how now.

The
eyes'
plain source
(light) of fact
can't be denied or
erased. But let doubt of vision
creep in and all is shadowed like planets the sun hides.

Dead

dead

you say

to yourself

as if to practice—

between shallow desperate breaths—

one word, one lifetime spent perfecting its solemn vow.

Ah
yes
Mimi
and her cold
hands: we'd take them up
in our own given half a chance,
but we can't. We must have distance in order to weep.

Cry

wild

as crows

on branches

heavy with snow, bent

against nothing more than the weight

of wilderness. Sorrow is light compared to this bold show.

Fore

told—

the fools

alone will

laugh—your sweetheart and

you in this sublime reunion.

Better tell the sky its violet hues presage mirth.

Be
long
as breath
deeply drawn,
be still as arrow
new-fletched, be the balanced cord pulled
taut by reason. Only here can peace find its true mark.

Vestige

These
songs
do not
guarantee
anything. Open
your hands as if to take away
the gift. No, open your palms to the reveling wind.

From
time
to time
the rubber
chicken shows up, cold
and yellow, slightly stiff, like a
punchline let slip in solemn talk. The god of death laughs.

All
things
sated
by shadow—
what shall we call you?
Flora and fauna of the mind,
welcome the bared sun, the desperate and brazen rain.

What
shall
Monday
bring? A loss,
duplicitous time,
the covers turned up trim and neat.
Just here we gave it all up—time, ourselves, the balance.

Where
else
but in
my black heart
could that anger rise.
The neighbors heard, you said, as if
there was shame in telling loud what I alone could speak.

Dig

deep

enough

and you'll find

proof of something said

that must have meant more than it seems,

must have meant something like 'Love' or 'Come back' or

'Yes, now.'

Mind—

rock—

made wet

by surprise—

glorious moment

of clarity and stillness bared

to the heavens, to the universe, to the deluge.

Rose

rose

open

lips and tongues

berry blossom banquet

twelve gifts arrived at the door

passed in by a mute stranger from the snowy front stoop.

Be-
hind
the trees
two deer walk
like shadow puppets,
their torsos still, only knees
lifted and set down in rhythmic certitude, heads high.

Short

cut

be damned.

Lovely wood

peckered by silence,

I'll find my lost self here below

new snow fall, the self cut short by what was circled round.

Snow

melts

on the

tongue of wind.

All song, these winter

days with sun decked out in cloud, wind

tonguing the reed of snow in syncopated rhythm.

Tried
true,
measured
absolute,
found both lacking
as if birds had only feathers
and no flight. Throats and no vestige of a cosmic song.

Grass

moves

toward

ripe water—

buffalo before

the rail trapped greed on the prairie,

haunches and horns and hooves' thundering—the rolling

herds.

No
doubt
we all
stand naked
on whatever day
closes out our era. Homo
sapiens, ignorant but clothed for an emperor.

We
can't
get too
close to them,
children ringing rosie,
skeletons of Freiburg rising
behind them. Ghosts on film. A plague of silent judges.

After a photograph by Werner Bischof

There
is
no here
here: only
horizon lifted
by corn and soybeans, all else
long ago buried by greed and unredeemable.

Not
here
ruins
or only
loss and memory—
gaunt shadows of what we should have
known about our savage selves. Remind us now again.

In our nation's capital, October 2004

Cloud's
heir:
thin masks
all seeming
now shell now pine cone
now our spiraling hearts: touch me,
touch me until this being of desire unwinds us.

Wild
thoughts
run east
carrying
mountains and glaciers
between their teeth. Who can listen,
in the Hamptons, when the chair umpire calls 'Love–Love.'

Ice

aims

toward

earth: naked

finger of borrowed

time, climate's collapse, our own souls

borrowed from earth's tainted finger, aiming toward ice.

Lake

of

my heart

—awestruck heart—

plangent and reedy,

no more shallow than alchemists'

dreams, now lead, now gold, now the temptation of terror.

Trust

wind

seed says

to tumble

your newly chafed heart.

How I long for water, the deep

drink. Carry me to the sea, my black sailor beckons.

Still
life:
onion
slantwise red
peeled to green, pale brie,
potato eyes behind shadow—
what brave design lies beneath—vanity or famine?

Breast,
palm,
shoulder,
the entire
dry inventory
met by stained sheets, scrubbed by loufah,
swollen, stiff, fallen, limp, catastrophe. Oh body!

Sun

sets

against

the plate glass—

Manhattan blushes

as if she'd stepped naked and cold

from the Hudson to find her robes nicked by hooligans.

Rain

reigns.

Be not

temperate.

The coconut guards

its white flesh in green robes and fur

and rides the rain like a padishah on a gilt horse.

Bug

walks

tip-toe

on water,

ruffles the surface.

Hurrah hurrah the leaves shout, we

are many, lapping, curling, fainter—hurry, count us!

So
seek
beauty—
all else is
false hope or blind faith.
What can be seen or heard or known
by pressing hard against this world—that is beautiful.

I
can
see, there.
Look, you too!
Too late, you missed it.
Now my heart beats, so long, so long.
Knowing this hurts. Two pelicans churned the floating
breeze.

And
all
waters
rise, subside—
study the loon, how
she leans into waves, then pulls back
before she enters the water. From a distance, calm.

Your
lips
balanced—
three petals—
oh moment of light
on my nipple. Make this all ways
a prayer for immortality: blessings on your tongue.